TULSA CITY-COUNTY LIBRARY

I'M THE BIGGEST!
IN THE DESERTS

LAURA K. MURRAY

CREATIVE EDUCATION · CREATIVE PAPERBACKS

CONT

4 Let's Explore the Desert!

6 Dry Ground

11 Long Roots

14 Animals, Big and Small

18 Full of Life

20
In the Deserts

22
Word Review

23
Read More & Websites

24
Index

LET'S EXPLORE THE DESERT!

The sun burns brightly overhead. The air is hot and dry. A tall saguaro (*sah-WAH-roh*) cactus grows nearby. Use your magnifying glass to inspect its **spines**.

spines - stiff, prickly parts of a cactus

Dry Ground

Deserts are the driest places on Earth. Animals and plants have **adapted** to live in the hot, dry conditions. They can survive with little water.

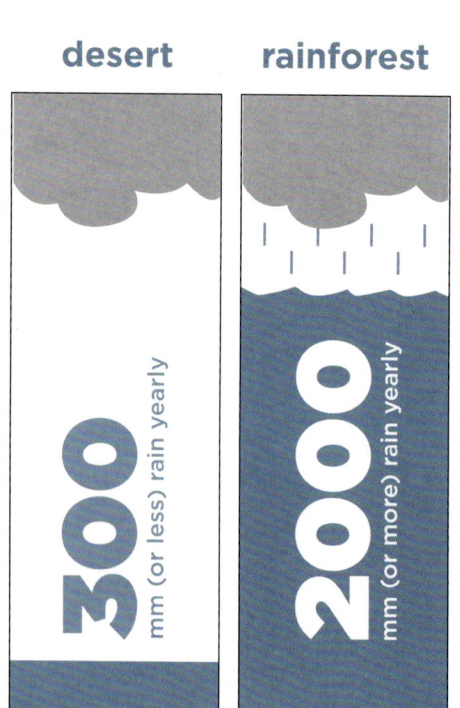

desert: 300 mm (or less) rain yearly
rainforest: 2000 mm (or more) rain yearly

adapted - changed to survive

The Sahara is the biggest hot desert in the world. It stretches across Africa. It covers 3.6 million square miles (9.3 million sq km). Farther south, the smaller Namib Desert has some of the world's tallest sand **dunes**.

dunes - hills of loose sand formed by the wind

Long Roots

Desert plants often have long root systems. Their roots may reach deep into the ground for water. Mesquite trees have the longest roots. Their **taproots** can grow more than 100 feet (30.5 m) deep. Other desert plants have shorter root systems.

taproots - main, downward-growing roots; smaller roots grow off a taproot

Most saguaro cactus roots grow just four inches (10.2 cm) deep. But they spread wide. They soak up moisture quickly. Cacti and other **succulents** store water in their stems, leaves, and roots.

succulents - plants with thick leaves and stems that store water

Animals, Big and Small

Camels are the biggest desert animals. They weigh up to 2,200 pounds (998 kg). They can be nearly seven feet (2.1 m) tall. Camels' eyelashes and nostrils keep out sand. Their humps store fat for energy.

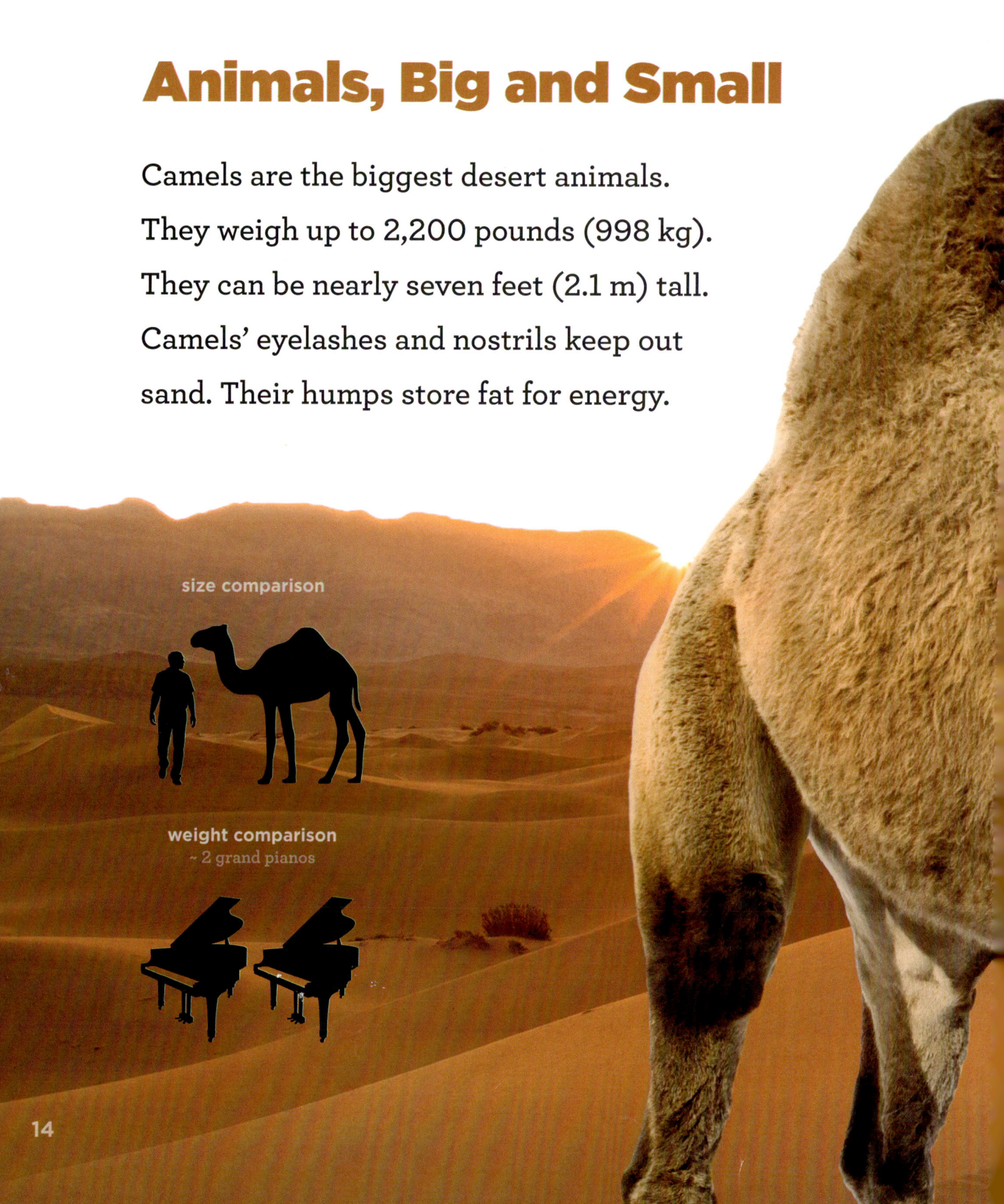

size comparison

weight comparison
~ 2 grand pianos

kangaroo rat
4.5 ounces (128 g)

Gila monster
5 pounds (2.3 kg)

Smaller animals live in the desert, too. The Gila monster weighs about five pounds (2.3 kg). This lizard stores fat in its tail. It can go months without eating. The kangaroo rat is even smaller. It weighs only four and a half ounces (128 g). It gets moisture from seeds rather than water.

Full of Life

From kangaroo rats to camels, deserts are full of life. What other amazing things can you discover about these hot, dry places?

fennec fox

kangaroo rat

19

IN THE DESERTS

Largest hot deserts in the world:

5
Great Victoria
134,650 sq mi

4
Kalahari
360,000 sq mi

3
Gobi
500,000 sq mi

2
Arabian
900,000 sq mi

1
Sahara
3.6 million sq mi

Word Review

Do you remember what these words mean? Look at the pictures for clues, and go back to the page where the words were defined, if you need help.

adapted page 6

dunes page 8

spines page 5

succulents page 13

taproots page 11

Read More

Heos, Bridget. *Do You Really Want to Visit a Desert?*
Mankato, Minn.: Amicus, 2015.

Schuetz, Kari. *Life in a Desert.*
Minneapolis: Bellwether Media, 2016.

Websites

National Geographic Kids: Desert
https://kids.nationalgeographic.com/explore/nature/habitats/desert/#deserts-camel-sahara.jpg
Read an article about the world's deserts.

World Biomes: Desert
http://kids.nceas.ucsb.edu/biomes/desert.html
Learn more about desert weather, plants, and animals.

Note: Every effort has been made to ensure that the websites listed above are suitable for children, that they have educational value, and that they contain no inappropriate material. However, because of the nature of the Internet, it is impossible to guarantee that these sites will remain active indefinitely or that their contents will not be altered.

Index

adaptations	6, 11, 13, 14, 17	**Gila monsters**	17
Africa	8, 21	**kangaroo rats**	17, 18
Namib Desert	8	**mesquite trees**	11
Sahara Desert	8, 21	**roots**	11, 13
cacti	5, 13	**sand dunes**	8
camels	14, 18	**water**	6, 11, 13

PUBLISHED BY CREATIVE EDUCATION AND CREATIVE PAPERBACKS

P.O. Box 227, Mankato, Minnesota 56002
Creative Education and Creative Paperbacks are imprints of The Creative Company
www.thecreativecompany.us

LIBRARY OF CONGRESS CATALOGING-IN-PUBLICATION DATA

Names: Murray, Laura K., author.
Title: In the deserts / Laura K. Murray.
Series: I'm the biggest.
Summary: From shortest to tallest and biggest to smallest, this ecosystem investigation uses varying degrees of comparison to take a closer look at the relationships of desert flora, fauna, and landforms.

Identifiers: ISBN 978-1-64026-060-3 (hardcover)
ISBN 978-1-62832-648-2 (pbk)
ISBN 978-1-64000-176-3 (eBook)
This title has been submitted for CIP processing under LCCN 2018938952.

CCSS: RI.1.1, 2, 4, 5, 6, 7; RI.2.1, 2, 5, 6, 7; RI.3.1, 2, 5, 7; RF.1.1, 3, 4; RF.2.3, 4

COPYRIGHT © 2019 CREATIVE EDUCATION, CREATIVE PAPERBACKS

International copyright reserved in all countries. No part of this book may be reproduced in any form without written permission from the publisher.

DESIGN AND PRODUCTION

by Joe Kahnke; art direction by Rita Marshall
Printed in the United States of America

PHOTOGRAPHS by Getty Images (Feifei Cui-Paoluzzo/Moment, Joel Sartore/National Geographic, Joel Sartore/National Geographic Photo Ark/National Geographic), iStockphoto (26ISO, 35007, chrisinthai, GlobalP, themacx), Minden Pictures (Michael D. Kern/NPL, Mary McDonald/NPL), Shutterstock (3000ad, aarrows, Johnny Adolphson, Rauf Aliyev, amenic181, apstockphoto, Nedim Bajramovic, chuyuss, Jakub Czajkowski, enterphoto, Dick Kenny, Aleksandra H. Kossowska, LifetimeStock, Felix Lipov, Oleg Lopatkin, Stephen Marques, N Mrtgh, orxy, Bahruz Rzayev, SonNumber4, SZBDesign, Daniel Zuppinger)

FIRST EDITION HC 9 8 7 6 5 4 3 2 1
FIRST EDITION PBK 9 8 7 6 5 4 3 2 1